자헌 이정자의 열세 번째 시조집(2023)

뿌리를 찾아서

이 정 자 지음

도서
출판 조은

뿌리를 찾아서 In Search of The Root

인쇄일 2023년 5월 20일
발행일 2023년 5월 25일
지은이 이정자
발행인 김화인
펴낸곳 도서출판 조은
편집인 김진순
주소 서울시 중구 을지로20길 12 대성빌딩 405호(인현동)
전화 (02)2273-2408
팩스 (02)2272-1391
출판등록 1995년 7월 5일 신고번호 제1995-000098호
ISBN 979-11-91735-59-8
정가 15,000원

♠ 잘못된 책은 바꾸어 드리겠습니다
♠ 이 책의 내용은 신저작권법에 의하여 국제적으로 보호받고 있습니다.
♠ 전재 및 복제를 할 수 없습니다.

뿌리를 찾아서 In Search of The Root

순 서 Contents

제1부 뿌리를 찾아 Part 1 In Search of The Root

단군왕검 Dangun Wanggeom ⋯ 14

양산촌장 알평공 Prince Alpyeong, Yangsan Village Headman ⋯ 15

표암재(瓢巖齋) Pyoamjae ⋯ 16

악강묘(嶽降廟) Akgangmyo ⋯ 18

고향1 Hometown 1 ⋯ 19

고향2 Hometown 2 ⋯ 20

추억1 Memories 1 ⋯ 21

추억2 Memories 2 ⋯ 23

맹모삼천의 교훈 Mencius Mother's Lesson ⋯ 24

고향 하늘 Home Sky ⋯ 27

아버지의 산 Father's Mountain ⋯ 29

어머니의 뜰 Mother's Garden ⋯ 31

고향3 - 귀한 만남 Precious Meeting ⋯ 33

무선정(武宣亭) Museonjeong ⋯ 34

충주호 사계 Chungju Lake Four Seasons ⋯ 36

다시 가꾼 師苑 Re-adorned Sawon ⋯ 39

제2부 자연의 노래 Nature's Song

자연과 살다 I live with nature ⋯ 42
나의 집, 우리 아파트 My House, My Apartment ⋯ 43
이 봄날을 지날까? Will this spring day pass? ⋯ 44
바다풍경1 Seascape 1 ⋯ 45
허심(虛心) Empty Heart ⋯ 46
흐뭇한 마음 Happy Heart ⋯ 47
농심1 Farmer's Heart 1 ⋯ 48
농심2 Farmer's Heart 2 ⋯ 49
행복1 Happiness 1 ⋯ 50
행복2 Happiness 2 ⋯ 51
풀꽃의 노래1 Flower's Song 1 ⋯ 52
풀꽃의 노래2 Flower's Song 2 ⋯ 53
주는 기쁨1 The Joy of Giving 1 ⋯ 54
주는 기쁨2 The Joy of Giving 2 ⋯ 55
전원을 가꾸며 Cultivate Field ⋯ 56

제3부 4계의 노래 Songs of the Four Seasons

봄비 Spring Rain ⋯ 60
패랭이꽃(석죽화) Gillyflower ⋯ 61
강처럼 산처럼 Like a Mountain Like a River ⋯ 62
오월 들녘 The Field of May ⋯ 63
오월은 May ⋯ 64
바다의 숨결 The Breath of The Sea ⋯ 65
바다풍경2 Seascape 2 ⋯ 66
저녁 바다 Evening Sea ⋯ 67
고향의 소리 The Sound of My Hometown ⋯ 68
고향의 향 Scent of Home ⋯ 69
가을 편지 Autumn Letter ⋯ 70
가을 하늘 The Autumn Sky ⋯ 71
성탄절 Christmas ⋯ 72
꿈꾸는 눈사람 Snow Man ⋯ 73
성탄의 기쁨을 모두에게 Christmas Joy to All ⋯ 74

제4부 여정의 쉼터 Journey

백두산 천지 Baekdu-Mountain Sky Pond … 78
병마총 Terracotta Warriors … 79
노르웨이 여정1 Norway Itinerary 1 … 80
노르웨이 여정2 Norway Itinerary 2 … 81
뉴욕 9.11 기념관 New York 9/11 Memorial … 82
뉴욕 지하철 풍경 New York Subway Scene … 83
아! 대설원 Ah! Great Snowfield … 84
나이아가라 폭포 Niagara Falls … 85
톤래샵 사람들 Tonlae Sap People … 86
앙코르 왓트 Angkor Wat … 87
푸쉬킨 동상 Pushkin Statue … 89
네바강 노을을 타고 Riding the Sunset on the Neva River … 90
대영 박물관 British Museum … 91
에펠탑(la Tour Eiffel) Eiffel Tower … 92
독일 고속도로 German Highway … 93
스위스 Swiss … 94
베네치아1 Venice 1 … 95
베네치아2 Venice 2 … 96
로마 Rome … 97
룩셈부르크 Luxembourg … 98
나라의 사슴 Deer in Nara … 99
라스베가스 Las Vegas … 100
그랜드 캐년 Grand Canyon … 101

제5부 일상의 소묘
Part 5 The lyricism of Everyday Life

초록이 비치네요 It's Green … 104
나비 정원 Butterfly Garden … 105
결국은 In the End … 106
기분 따라 Follow the Mood … 107
Beautiful Relaxing Music을 들으며 Listening to Beautiful Relaxing Music … 108
춤추는 능소화 Dancing Trumpet Creeper … 109
신독(愼獨) Be Careful When Alone … 110
현대인의 나이 Modern Age … 111
고향의 향 Scent of Home … 112
영상을 보며 Watching the Video … 113
Tim Janis의 영상 음악을 감상하며 Listening to the Video Music of Tim Janis … 114
공평한 기다림 The Fair Wait … 115
카톡이 생명 Kakao Talk is Life … 116
시조의 세계화 Globalization of Sijo … 117
송구영신 Welcome the New Year … 118
부활의 아침 Resurrection Morning … 120

부록: 저자의 문단 경력 및 저서 기타 … 124
Appendix: Author's Paragraph Career and Other Publications

시인의 말

　2022년 1월 5일에 제11.12시조집 『문득 바라본 창밖 그림』과 『눈을 들어 산을 보라』를 합본으로 출간했다. 본 시조집 『뿌리를 찾아서』는 예기치 않게 원로 문인을 배려하는 정부 지원을 받게 되어 13번째 시조집으로 출간하게 되었다. 이번 시조집은 학문과 함께 시인으로서 살아온 나의 자전적인 색채가 많이 곁들어 있다. 22년 12월에 연락을 받고 몇 개월 동안의 준비기간이기에 처음부터 주제별로 계획을 세워서 시작(詩作)을 하고 정리했다.

　먼저 뿌리를 생각하게 되었다. 10여년 전 문정공 『이달충 문집 연구』를 쓸 때 경주 표암산을 찾아 관리인의 안내로 두루 살펴보았다. 그 후 경주에 가면 의례 찾아 가곤 했다. 제정공(霽亭公) 산소는(경북 안동시 풍산면 만운동) '이달충 문학연구서'를 종친회에 전할 때 10월 시제(時祭)때 가기도 했다. 그래서 그간 한 번도 시작(詩作)에서 언급하지 않은 뿌리인데 시조 작품으로 뿌리를 찾게 되었다.
　두 번째는 몇 년 전부터 우리 부부가 스스로 가꾸어 먹으면서 경험한 농사 초보자로서의 농심(農心)에 대해 썼다. 곧 자연의 노래이다.
　세 번째는 '자연의 노래'와 함께 하는 자연과의 대화이며 자연과 함께하는 '삶'에 대해 썼다. 곧 4계의 노래이다.
　네 번째는 그간 우리 부부가 함께 간 세계여행에서 보고

듣고 느낀 시편들을 다시 일부 쓰고 정리했다. 곧 여정의 쉼터이다.

다섯 번째는 요즘 나의 일상에서 느끼고 만나는 소재들로 구성했다.

이렇게 주제별로 나누어 하나하나 쓰고 정리하다 보니 시조 1권 분량이 나왔다. 감사할 뿐이다. 밤 10시부터 2시까지가 고요한 나만의 시간이다. 논문을 쓰듯이 하나하나 새기며 작품을 썼다. 그 가운데 '몇 수'는 기 발표된 작품임을 밝힌다.

시와 시조계에 몇 명의 귀한 문우 제자들이 있다. 이번 정부 지원을 받게 된 것은 '풀꽃 동인'들의 성원 덕택이다. 20여년 전 건국대에서 인연을 맺은 시인들로 한결같은 마음으로 모임을 하고 매년 동인지 『풀꽃』을 출간한다.

시력 30여년의 결실은 나를 돌아보며 한 편 한 편 썼기에 나의 자전적 단면이 다분히 있다. 그것이 나의 일생의 일부이기도 하다. 어차피 '시작(詩作)'은 작가의 마음의 풍경이고 작가의 분신이기도 하다. 독자들께 다가가며 -. 감사한다.

    2023. 5. 15 자헌 이정자(慈軒 李靜子)

Jaheon Lee Jeongja's 13th Sijo Collection (2023)

In Search of The Root
Written by Jeongja Lee

Poet's Words

　On January 5, 2022, the 11th and 12th collection of poems 『Pictures outside the Window that I Suddenly Looked at』 and 『Raise My Eyes and Look at the Mountains』 were published as a combined book. This collection of sijo,
　『In Search of The Root』, was unexpectedly published as the 13th collection of sijo, receiving government support that is considerate of elder writers. This collection of poems contains many of my autobiographical colors, which have been lived as a poet along with academic studies. I was contacted in December 22, and since it was a preparation period for several months, I made a plan by topic from the beginning, started writing poetry, and organized it.
　First, I thought of my roots. About 10 years ago, when I was writing 『Lee Dalchung Anthology Research』, I visited Mt.Pyoam. After that, when

I went to Gyeongju, I would go to the ceremony. JeJeong-gong(霽亭公)Sanso(Manun-dong,Pungsan-myeon,Andong-si, Gyeongsangbuk-do) also attended the festival in October when I delivered "Lee Dal-chung's Literary Research Book" to the family meeting. So, it is a root that has never been mentioned in poetry writing, but I found the root as a sijo work.

Second, I wrote about farmer's mind (農心) as a beginner in farming that my husband and I experienced while growing and eating for ourselves a few years ago. It's nature's song

The third is a conversation with nature with 'nature's song' and wrote about 'life' with nature. Soon it is 'the four season's song'.

Fourth, I rewrote and organized the things that my husband and I had seen, heard, and felt during our world travel together. It is soon the shelter for the journey.

The fifth is composed of the materials that I feel and encounter in my daily life these days.

As I divided them into topics and wrote and organized them one by one, I came up with one volume of Sijo. I am just grateful. From 10:00 pm to 2:00 am is my quiet time. As if writing a thesis,

I wrote my work by engraving each one. Among them, 'a few works' are already published works.

There are several precious literary disciples in the world of poetry and sijo. It is thanks to the support of the 'coterie' that this government support was received. Poets who made a relationship at Konkuk University more than 20 years ago gather together with a consistent mind and publish a coterie magazine 「Grass Flower」 every year.

The fruit of more than 30 years as poet is that I wrote one by one while looking back at myself, so there is a lot of my autobiographical aspect. It is also a part of my life. After all, 'poetry' is the landscape of the poet's mind and also the poet's alter ego. Approaching readers －. Thank you.

2023. 5. 15 Jaheon, Jeongja Lee

제1부

뿌리를 찾아서

단군왕검
양산촌장 알평공
표암재(瓢巖齋)
악강묘(嶽降廟)
고향1
고향2
추억1
추억2
맹모삼천의 교훈
고향 하늘
아버지의 산
어머니의 뜰
고향3
무선정(武宣亭)
충주호 사계
다시 가꾼 師苑

단군왕검

환인이 환웅 낳아
단군이 태어나니

단군은 아사달에
나라를 세웠었지

단군은 하나님 후손
한민족의 시조다.

Dangun Wanggeom

Hwanin gave birth to Hwanung,
Dangun was born from Hwanung.

Dangun in Asadal,
founded the Chosun country.

Dangun is the descendent of God,
He is Korean ancestor.

양산촌장 알평공

신라의 육촌(六村)중에
양산촌장 알평(謁平)공은

표암봉 내려와서
신라 개국 공신이다

이분도 하늘의 후손
경주이씨 시조다.

Prince Alpyeong, Yangsan Village Headman

The six villages of Silla,
Alpyeong, Head of Yangsan Village,

He came down on Pyoam-Peak,
the member of Silla's founding.

Alpyeong too is the scion of Heaven,
The founder of Gyeongju Yi clan.

표암재(瓢巖齋)

기천년 흘렀어도
표암재 춘계향사

신라의 건국원훈(建國元勳)
이알평공(李謁平公) 배향(配享)이라

신라의 화백제도가
표암재서 싹텄다.

* 경주이씨 시조를 모시는 사당인 악강묘(嶽降廟)와 제사를 준비하는 공간인 표암재(瓢巖齋)가 있다.
  경주시(慶州市) 동천동(東川洞) 소재(所在). 표암선생(瓢巖先生) 진한(辰韓) 알천(閼川) 양산촌장(楊山村長) 신라(新羅) 건국원훈(建國元勳) 문조공(文祖公) 이알평(李謁平)을 배향(配享). 경북기념물 제54호로 지정.

Pyoamjae (瓢巖齋)

Even if over 2,000 years,
Pyoamjae Spring Festival.

Silla's Founding Contributor (建國元勳)
Yi Al Pyeong has been enshrined (配享)

It sprouted from the Pyoamjae
Silla's Hwabaek System too.

* There is Akgangmyo, a shrine for the ancestor of the Gyeongju Lee family, and Pyoamjae, a space for preparing ancestral rites.
  Located in Dongcheon-dong, Gyeongju-si. Pyoam, Jinhan, Alcheon, Yangsan village chief, Silla, Founding Contributor, Munjogong, Lee Alpyeong (配享). A meritorious retainer at the founding of Silla

악강묘(嶽降廟)

악강묘 경주이씨
혈맥의 근원이며

육촌장 화백회의
신라 건국 완성하니

표암재 화백회의는
민주정치 발상지.

Akgangmyo

Akgangmyo is the source of
the Gyeongju Yi clan's bloodline.

Six village head Hwabaek meeting
completed the founding of Silla

Pyoamjae Hwabaek Conference
is birthplace of democracy.

고향1

대구시 덕산동은
태어나서 자라던 곳

칠곡군 행정동은
약동초등 다니던 곳

또다시 회귀한 고향
중고등은 대구다.

Hometown 1

Deoksan-dong, in Daegu is
where I was born and raised.

Chilgok-gun Haengjeong-dong is
where graduated primary school

The city of returned again,
middle and high school are Daegu.

고향2

남편의 본적 따라
본적이 서울이니

내 고향 서울일까?
자녀들은 서울인데

아니지, 제2고향은
서울이라 하겠지.

Hometown 2

According to the husband
my hometown is Seoul.

My children's hometown is Seoul.
Is my hometown really Seoul?

Not at all, my second hometown
would probably be Seoul.

추억1

그때엔 보릿고개 동냥하러 많이 왔다
어머닌 심부름을 나에게 시키셨다
그들은 "복 받을 거요"라며 축복 인사 꼭 했다.

그 말이 듣기 좋아 스스로 즐겨했고
엄마의 바쁜 일손 스스로 도우면서
뒷밭의 부식 거리도 내가 따서 오곤 했다

뒷밭에 가는 길은 아침이슬 가득했고
밭둑에 나팔꽃이 너무나 아름다워
한참을 넋 잃은 듯이 바라보곤 했었다.

지금도 또렷하게 기억에 남는 것은
어린 맘 풍요롭게 감성을 키워준 건
밭둑에 곱게 피어난 아름다운 나팔꽃.

Memories 1

At that time, many beggars

came in March and April.
My mother made me that errand
"give them a bowl of rice"
They said me "you will be much blessed"
They always congratulated me.

I was glad to hear that, so
I enjoyed errands myself.
Even my mother's busy work,
I diligently helped her.
I used to pick side dishes from
vegetables in the backyard.

The road to the backyard
was full of morning dew.
The morning glory on the field bank
is so beautiful flower.
I used to look at the flower
like I was lost for a long time.

Even now, what I still remains
in my mind apparently,
The thing that enriched my young
and nurtured my emotions,
Several morning glory bloomed
beautifully on the field bank.

추억2 : 가투놀이

문예반 친구들과
모이면 가투놀이

초중장 읽어주면
종장 찾기 바빴으니

놀이도 재밌는 경쟁
시조 백 편 외웠다.

Memories 2: Gatu play

Meeting with literary mates,
we enjoyed Gatu play.

When one person read the first line
the other friends looked for the last.

Because play was a competition too,
I memorized Sijo 100 then.

맹모삼천의 교훈

우리 집 이사한 건 순전히 오빠 따라
원래는 대구지만 일제 말 고향으로
초등은 아버지의 고향 시골에서 다녔다.

오빠의 학교 따라 대구로 이사왔다.
덕택에 나도 따라 대구에서 공부했다
오빠가 서울 오면서 덩달아 또 서울로

이렇게 오빠 따라 공부를 하다보니
자연히 따라따라 하는 습관 몸에 배어
저절로 공부를 하여 박사까지 되었다.

초딩땐 시골에서 공부와는 담을 쌓지
밤이면 모여앉아 뜨개질이 공부였고
낮에는 동생이 없어 혼자 놀이 즐겼지.

그러다 대구 오니 주위엔 온통 공부
나 또한 오빠 따라 공부를 하였지만
결국엔 맹모삼천이 나를 키운 가르침.

Mencius Mother's Lesson

My family moved the house
following my elder brother
originally Daegu,
but moving to hometown.
I went to elementary school
in the hometown of my father.

My family moved to Daegu
following my eld brother's school.
Thanks to my eld brother
I studied in Daegu.
We moved to Seoul again when
my eld brother goes to Seoul.

I was studying like this
with my elder brother.
The habit of following
is ingrained in the body.
I studied harder on my own
and became a doctor.

When elementary school,
I did'nt study in my hometown.
At night, we gathered together
and studied knitting.
During day, I enjoyed playing alone
because no my younger sister.

When I came to Daegu,
all around me was studying.
I also studied following
my brother naturerally
However, it is the teaching
that Mencius' mother raised me.

고향 하늘

찾아온 고향하늘
감회가 깊은 것은

유년에 그려보던
파아란 캔버스에

두둥실 마음을 띄워
그 시절을 새긴다.

어릴 적 그 하늘이
그대로 다가오니

공간이 자연스레
시간을 돌려놓고

마음은 유년을 향해
온 가족을 만난다.

Home Sky

What is deeply felt is
the hometown sky that I have come to.

I draw in my childhood
on blue sky canvas.

Dudungsil, I am floated my heart
and remember those days.

The sky when I was young
is coming as it is.

Space is naturally
turnning back old time to present.

My old heart toward my childhood
meets the whole family then.

아버지의 산

살다가 힘들 때도 넘어지고 싶을 때도
언제나 그 자리에 변치 않고 지켜 준 건
내 곁에 우뚝 서 있는
아버지의 산이었다.

바란 것 어긋나서 실망 속에 있을 때도
허한 맘 다독이며 힘을 주던 그 말씀에
세상을 지켜보면서
절제하는 내가 됐다.

아버지 깊은 뜻을 지금에야 알 것 같아
나 또한 아이에게 다독이고 힘을 주어
그 옆에 조용히 서서
쉬어 가는 산이 되리.

Father's Mountain

Even time when my life is hard,
when I want to fall down,
the thing that always stayed in that
place without changing,
that standing taller next to me,
It was my father's mountain.

Even time when I'm in despair
for I didn't get what I wanted,
In the words that comforted
my heart and gave me strength,
watching that the world around me
I became the self-restraint.

I think I understand now
the deep meaning of my father.
I also comfort my children
and I will encourage them.
Beside them I am standing quietly
and will be a mountain of rest.

어머니의 뜰

어머닌 별당 아씨 시절을 품으셨다.
조부께 글 배우고 내훈으로 익히셨던
그 시절 평생 새기며 조신(操身)하게 사셨다.

여헌(旅軒)의 후손임을 학덕으로 자부하며
온 동네 사돈지(査頓紙)는 어머니의 작품이고
외조부 소상 제문(祭文)엔 조상 은덕 밝히셨다.

어머니 익히셨던 내훈(內訓)을 꺼내보고
어머니 향이 묻은 구절구절 살펴보다
잠들면 어머니 모습 꿈속에서 반긴다.

Mother's Garden

My mother raised her dreams
in her gardenbuildings as a girl.
She learned how to read and write
from her grandfather when a girl.
In those days, by girlhood education
she lived discreetly her whole life.

She's a descendant of Yeoheon(旅軒),
proud of his academic virtues.
She had written Sadon-letters(查頓紙)
of her neighborhood women.
She had written the memorial,
the virtues of her ancestors.

Even now, I see the home precept
that my mother had kept.
I examine each and every phrase
that smells like mother's scent.
In my dreams when I fall asleep,
my mom welcomes me with two arms.

고향3 - 귀한 만남

충주에 내려온 지
삼십 성상 가까운데

이웃과 만남 없어
이웃은 모르지만

문우들 귀한 만남은
고향보다 가깝다.

Precious Meeting

It has been nearly 30 years
since I came down to Chungju.

I don't meet the neighbors well
and so I don't know my neighbors.

However, the writing friends's meeting
is closer than hometown friends.

무선정(武宣亭)

충주성 한 자락에 꼭꼭 숨긴 탄약 창고
화약을 제조했던 최무선을 기리려고
울창한 숲속 개울 옆 무선정을 세웠다.

사람은 유한해도 그 업적은 영원한 것
충신의 애국심은 세월 함께 젖어 들어
정자(亭子)에 새겨진 글로 그의 뜻을 살핀다.

Museonjeong

An ammunition warehouse
hidden in Chungju Castle.
To honor Mu-seon Choi,
who made gunpowder
Museonjeong (武宣亭)was built next to a stream
in the dense forest of mountains.

People are finite, but
their achievements are eternal.
Patriotism of loyal subjects
is soaked with time.
His meaning can be known by the writing
engraved on the pavilion.

충주호 사계

(서시)
산 좋고 물 맑으며 맘씨 좋은 충주에는
충주성 이름답게 발 닿으면 명승지라
그중에 충주호 사계는 부담 없이 가는 곳.

(봄)
개나리 진달래꽃 철쭉꽃이 만발하고
현란한 벚꽃잎은 나비처럼 휘날리고
호수는 햇살을 싣고 무지개로 일렁인다.

(여름)
사계절 푸른 숲을 물안개로 감싸 안고
드넓은 가슴으로 유람선을 띄우고서
호수는 바람을 타고 은사슬을 가른다.

(가을)
곱게 물든 가을 산이 머리 위에 드리울 땐
싱그런 초록 마음 다소곳이 접으면서
호수는 물길을 따라 긴 사색에 잠긴다.

(겨울)
화사한 눈꽃으로 덮여버린 겨울 산은
흰나비 춤사위로 현란하게 휘날리고
호수는 화공이 되어 수채화를 그린다.

Chungju Lake Four Seasons

(preface)
where the mountains are good,
the water's clear, and the heart's good
True to the name of Chungjuseong
it is a scenic spot.
Among them, Chungju Lake is a place
to go without any burden.

(Spring)
Forsythia, royal azaleas
and azaleas are in full bloom
Dazzling cherry blossom
petals flutter like butterflies
The lake shines with a pretty rainbow
as the sunshine is on it.

(summer)
Water mist embraces the green
forest for all the four season
The lake is floated a cruise ship
as a broader chest of its
The lake rides the refreshing wind

and runs through the silver chain.

(autumn)
When the finely colored autumn
mountains hang over my head
When my green heart full of fresh dreams
gets submerged in the lake
The calm lake flows along waterway
immersed in contemplation.

(winter)
Winter mountains covered
with bright beautiful snowflakes,
It flutters dazzlingly
with the dance of white butterflies
The calm lake becomes a painter
and draws watercolors oneself.

다시 가꾼 師苑
 – 졸업 60주년 기념문집을 보며

60주년 기념문집 낸 학교가 또 있을까?
고맙다 '다시 가꾼 사원(師苑)'을 읽게 되어,
장하다 동창들이여 탑 하나 또 세웠네

청운의 꿈을 안고 공부에 매진하던
그 시절, 추억으로 따스하게 다가오니
힘겹던 지난 시간도 감사하며 새긴다. ♣

* 사원(師苑)'은 대구사범학교(대구교육대학교 전신) 교지(校誌)였다
  졸업 60주년 기념문집 표제가 '다시 가꾼 師苑'이다.
* 코로나로 60주년 행사는 못했다.
* K 도지사를 비롯해 장군, 기업인, 교수 등 성공한 남자 동기들이 많아 졸업 50주년도 대구 G호텔에서 잘 치루었다.

Re-adorned Sawon(師苑)
– Looking at the 60th anniversary of graduation

Is there another school that
published the book for the 60th
(anniversary of graduation)?
Thank you for reading the book
that we made again.
Alumni, we all have a great job
we all built a great tower.

I was devoted to my studies
with a dream of blue luck.
The memories of those days
warmly come to me today.
Oh! thank God and welcome those days
even in the difficult times. ♣

제2부
자연의 노래

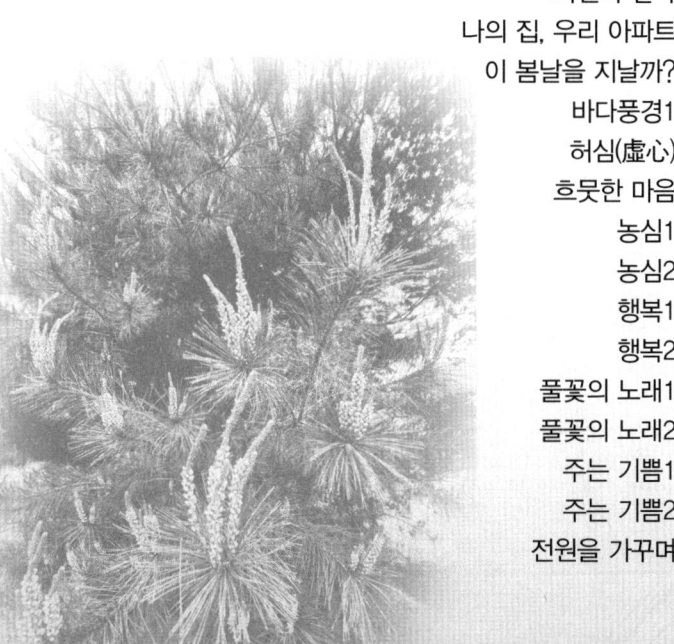

자연과 살다
나의 집, 우리 아파트
이 봄날을 지날까?
바다풍경1
허심(虛心)
흐뭇한 마음
농심1
농심2
행복1
행복2
풀꽃의 노래1
풀꽃의 노래2
주는 기쁨1
주는 기쁨2
전원을 가꾸며

자연과 살다

자연과 친교하니 생각도 맑아진다

푸르른 산도 좋고 개울물 더욱 좋다

세상의 명예쯤이야 자연속에 묻힌다.

I live with nature

I am closing with nature
so my thoughts is becomed clean.

The green mountains are good,
the stream water is even better.

The honor of the world in the dust
is forgotten in nature.

나의 집, 우리 아파트

산책길 아래에는
개울물이 흘러가고

울타리 장미꽃은
향기 실어 날아들고

나의 집
우리 아파트
살기 좋은 곳이다.

My House, My Apartment

A clean creek flows under
the promenade of apartment.

Hedge roses carry their scent
and fly away to my home.

My old home, LG apartment
is a very good place to live.

이 봄날을 지날까?

새소리 청량(淸亮)하게
정원에서 들려오고

봄볕이 따사롭게
내 시심(詩心)을 적셔오니

시 한 수 아니 올리고
이 봄날을 지날까?

Will this spring day pass?

I can hear the birds chirping
on the tree in the garden .

The warm spring sun light drenches
my poetic heart softly.

How can I pass this warm spring day
without composing a poem?

바다풍경 1

한나절 바닷새와
벗이 되어 훨훨 날고

푸르른 캠퍼스에
추억 한 점 올려놓고

창공에
그림 그린 듯
펼쳐지는 수채화.

Seascape 1

Half a day with seabirds
I become friends and fly away

On the green campus
I put a memory on it

At the sky
like a drawing painting
watercolor is spreading.

허심(虛心)

허심(虛心)이 자리하니
매사가 평안하다

주어진 일을 해도
도움 손길 넘쳐나고

건강이 따라와 주니
나이쯤은 잊는다

Empty Heart:

Where empty heart lies
everything is peaceful.

even if I do the job
helping hands overflow.

Health follows to me naturelly
I forget about my age.

흐뭇한 마음

전원을 가꾸면서
흐뭇한 이 마음은

심은 것 무럭무럭
자라는 그 모습에

커가는 아이를 보듯
뿌듯함을 느낀다.

Happy Heart

I am very happy heart
while cultivate a plant garden.

What I planted grow very well
seeing from the way those grow.

Like watching a child grow up well,
I feel proud from which plants grow.

농심1

밭갈이 초년생에
농사 방법 익혀준다.

고라니 오는 길엔
튼실하게 울을 치고

어린싹 가꾸는 정성
아이 보듯 살핀다.

Farmer's Heart 1

In the first year plowing the field,
he teaches how to farm to me.

I put up a strong fence
on the way to the elk deer.

Devotion to nurture young shoots,
I take care of like my child.

농심2

밤사이 잘도 자란
풍성한 상추 삼과

자르르 윤기나는
호박부침 한 접시에

농심은 흐뭇한 마음
자부심도 충만해.

Farmer's Heart 2

The lettuce grew well overnight.
The table is full of lettuce.

The cucumbers are shiny.
I made a zucchini fries.

The farmer is very happy
and full of pride with doing.

행복1

부모는 자식 덕에
행복을 만끽한 듯

초보자 농사일에
자녀들이 다녀갔다.

방학이 오자 무섭게
손주들도 다 왔다.

Happiness 1

Parents enjoy happiness
because of their son and daughter.

They visited their parents
to see their parents' farm work

As soon as their vacation came
all the grandchildren came too.

행복 2

나누는 기쁨 속에
행복도 따라오네

여름내 땀 흘리며
가꿔 온 수고 덕에

오늘은 복지관 들려
수확물을 드렸지.

Happiness 2

In the joy of sharing with you
happiness naturally follows.

Sweating in all the summer
thanks to the very hard work.

We go to the welfare center
to give the harvest things today.

풀꽃의 노래1

뉘 아니 보아줘도
스스로 잘 자라고

이 들녘 가득한 꽃
풀꽃들의 잔치이죠

벌 나비
모여든 자리
풍년가를 울려요.

Flower's Song 1

Even if you don't look at us
we grow well by itself.

This field is full of flowers
It is the feast of flowers.

In place where
bees and butterflies gather
we sing the song of abundance.

풀꽃의 노래 2

장미의 향기만큼
탐스런 모란만큼

자태와 향기만은
그들보다 못하여도

이 들녘
가득한 풀꽃
네가 진정 주인이다.

Flower's Song 2

As much as the scent of a rose
as much as the peony,

though you are inferior to them
in appearance and aroma,

this wide field
is full of grass flowers.
you are the sincere master.

주는 기쁨1

장마와 나들이로
며칠 만에 찾은 밭은

잡초가 자란 만큼
수확 또한 풍성하다

한가득 풀어놓고는
전화번호 누른다.

The Joy of Giving 1

Rainy season and outing
the field I found in a few days

as much as weeds grow well
the harvest is bountiful too.

Laying down abundent harvest
I dial the phone number.

주는 기쁨 2

앞집도 모르고 산
아파트 생활에서

소통의 매개체로
수확의 기쁨 보며

아파트 문이 열리니
고향 인심 느낀다.

The Joy of Giving 2

I didn't even know the house
of the front in apartment life

as a medium of communication
Seeing the joy of harvest

Opening the apartment door
I feel the heart of hometown.

전원을 가꾸며

전원을 가꾸면서 도연명을 그려본다
자연의 품속에서 나물 뜯고 풀 뽑으며
스스로 가꾸어 먹는 호사함을 즐긴다

어릴 적 소풍가듯 김밥을 챙겨갖고
모처럼 찾은 밭은 잡초조차 아름다워
노란 꽃 보라꽃들이 골골마다 가득하다

어떻게 잡초라고 마구갈아 엎을 건가
이렇게 아름답게 고운 꽃을 피웠는데
눈으로 즐기는 것만도 제 한 몫을 다한 걸

시들지 않는 꽃이 어디에 있었던가
스스로 자연으로 돌아가게 남겨두자
공동의 생명체로서 자유롭게 두고 보자.

Cultivate Field

While cultivating the garden,
I miss poet To Yeon-myeong.
Picking herbs and pulling grass
in the bosom of nature,
we enjoy the luxury of
self-cultivation eating.

Like going on a picnic ,
we take gimbap to go the field.
The field we found in a few days,
even the weeds are beautiful.
Red flowers, yellow and purple
flowers are full of valleys.

How are you going to do.
Does it overthrow as a weed?
They bloomed beautiful flower
in this wide and peaceful field.
I think so that they did their part
just by enjoying it with eyes.

Where was the unfading flower.
All the flowers bloom then wither.
Let themselves go back to
nature no man plow them.
Let us them be free to let themselves
as the common life form.

제3부
4계의 노래

봄비
패랭이꽃(석죽화)
강처럼 산처럼
오월 들녘
오월은
바다의 숨결
바다풍경2
저녁 바다
고향의 소리
고향의 향
가을 편지
가을 하늘
성탄절
꿈꾸는 눈사람
성탄의 기쁨을 모두에게

봄비

똑 똑 똑 조심스레
창문을 두드리다

살며시 다가와서
속삭이며 하는 말이

일어나 정원을 갈고
꽃씨 뿌려 두어요.

Spring Rain

Knock Knock Knock carefully,
spring rain knocks on the window.

The spring rain comes closer to me
and tell me whispering words.

You wake up, plowing the garden,
sowing the flower seeds please.

패랭이꽃(석죽화)

호젓한 들길에는
햇살도 따사롭고

소슬한 바람결에
다가온 너의 향기

지나던
발길 돌리고
네 자태에 머문다.

Gillyflower

On a secluded field road
the sunlight is warmer too.

In the gentle breeze of the spring
your aroma approached me.

Turn my steps
passing through that place
I appreciate your figure.

강처럼 산처럼

강물이 흘러가도
어제이고 오늘이듯

시간이 흘러가도
산들은 그대로 듯

젊음도
강산을 닮아
그대로면 좋겠네

Like a Mountain Like a River

Even if the river flows
like yesterday and today,

even if time passes
the mountains does not change,

youth also
as a river or mountain
I hope it stays the same.

오월 들녘

푸르른 오월 들녘
초록 바다 푸른 물결

스치는 바람 따라
파도처럼 출렁이고

삐리리
보리피리가
유년으로 달리네.

The Field of May

The green fields of May are
the green sea, the blue waves.

It sways like waves of east sea
following the passing wind.

Piri-ri
an oaten pipe is
running to the childhood.

오월은

오월은 신록의 달
오월은 축제의 달

싱그런 꿈을 싣고
젊음은 비상한다

태양도
오색 꿈 실어
찬란하게 빛나네.

May

May is the month of fresh green
May is the month of festivals.

Youth soars toward the dream
with carrying a fresh dream.

The sun too
shines more brilliantly
carrying a five-colored dream.

바다의 숨결

세차게 밀려가고
밀려오는 파도 소리

가만히 귀 기울어
나긋이 들어보면

파도는
바다의 숨결
숨을 쉬고 있다네

The Breath of The Sea

Being pushed very hard
the sound of crashing waves.

If I listen carefully
and listen to it silently.

The waves is
the breath of the sea,
the sea is breathing without rest.

바다풍경2

윤슬로 일렁이는
은빛 바다 그 너머로

선율이 펼쳐지는
아스라한 꽃 빛 연주

눈부신
모래밭에서
고운 시를 읊는다.

Seascape 2

Shimmering with effulgence
beyond the silver sea

The melody unfolds
with shady flower light play

I compose
the beautiful poem
on the dazzling fine sand.

저녁 바다

해거름 땅거미가
바닷가에 내려오면

갈매기 꺼~억 꺼~억
저녁 인사 나누면서

오늘도
참 좋은 하루
내일 다시 만나요

Evening Sea

When the sun goes down to the west,
dusk comes down to the beach.

Seagulls are kind to each other,
they say goodbye to the evening.

Today too
what a happy day
let see us again tomorrow.

고향의 소리

해거름 땅거미가
산등성을 내려오면

소모는 아이들의
왁자지껄 이랴~이랴~

더불어
쇠풍경 소리
저녁놀에 물든다

The Sound of My Hometown

When the sun goes down to the west,
dusk comes down to the ridge.

The sound of cowboys herding cattle
the clamorous sound 'hey, hey ~'.

Together,
the sound of cow bells
is dyed in the evening glow.

고향의 향

꽃처럼 아름다운
빨갛게 익은 감과

돌담을 돌아들면
구수한 숭늉 냄새

아련한
고향의 향이
가을볕에 따습다.

Scent of Home

Red very ripe persimmons
are beautiful as flowers

When I go around the stone wall
the savory smell of Sungnyung,

Like dreamy
the scent of hometown
is warm in the autumn sun.

가을 편지

오색의 단풍잎을
책갈피에 끼워 넣고

릴케의 시 읊으며
이 가을을 노래하면

마음은
갈바람 타고
추억 동산 달린다.

Autumn Letter

I put it in the bookmark
the five colored maple leaves.

Reciting the poem by Rilke
when I sing this autumn,

my own heart
rides the autumn wind;
running the garden of memory.

가을 하늘

댕그랑 울릴 듯한
유리알 캔버스에

저리도 고운 빛깔
어떻게 올렸을까

백합화
한 송이 올려
곱게 그린 정물화.

The Autumn Sky

The autumn sky dangling
on the glass bead canvas,

such a beautiful color,
how did it upload on the sky.

The lily,
one flower on the cloud
finely painted the still life.

성탄절

아이들 어릴 때는
온 식구 한맘으로

추리를 장식하며
선물까지 챙겼는데

지금은
카카오톡에
성탄 카드 올리네.

Christmas

When children are young
with the whole family as one,

Decorating the Christmas tree
I also prepared the gifts.

Nowadays
on Kakao Talk
I'm posting the Christmas card.

꿈꾸는 눈사람

새하얀 눈꽃 모자
깊숙이 눌러쓰고

눈사람 꼼짝 않고
사색에 잠겨있네

동화속
왕자님으로
승화하는 꿈꾸나?

Snow Man

Snowman put on pressing deeply
with pure white snowflower hat

The snowman stands motionless
he is lost in meditation

As a prince
in the fairy tale,
do you dream of sublimation?

성탄의 기쁨을 모두에게

외로이 홀로되어 쪽방에서 살아가는
연약한 노인들의 허기진 가슴에도
성탄의 충만한 은혜 빛이 되게 하소서

부모가 떠난 자리 굳세게 살아가는
외로운 소녀 소년 가장들의 가슴에도
성탄의 깊은 의미가 새겨지게 하소서

어려운 경제 사정 직장 잃은 가정에도
성탄의 기쁜 소식 구원의 손길 뻗어
한 줄기 찬란한 빛이 솟아나게 하소서

국가를 경영하는 정치인의 가슴에도
경제를 이어가는 기업인의 마음에도
성탄의 참된 진리로 깨어나게 하소서.

Christmas Joy to All

Old people being lonely
and living in a small room,
Christmas joy even in the hungry
hearts of frail old people,
Let it be the light of Christmas
the full grace of Christmas.

The boys and girls living strong
where their parents left away,
Christmas meaning even in
the hearts of lonely girls and boys,
Let it be the deep meaning of Lord;
Christmas be engraved their heart.

Difficult economic life,
families who have lost their jobs,
The good news of Christmas
extends the hand of salvation,
Let it be a ray of brilliant light
Let it be the light of hope.

Even in the hearts of statesman
who administer the country,
Even in the minds of people
who continue the economy,
Let it be waking up their dreams
with the real truth of Christmas.

제4부
여정의 쉼터

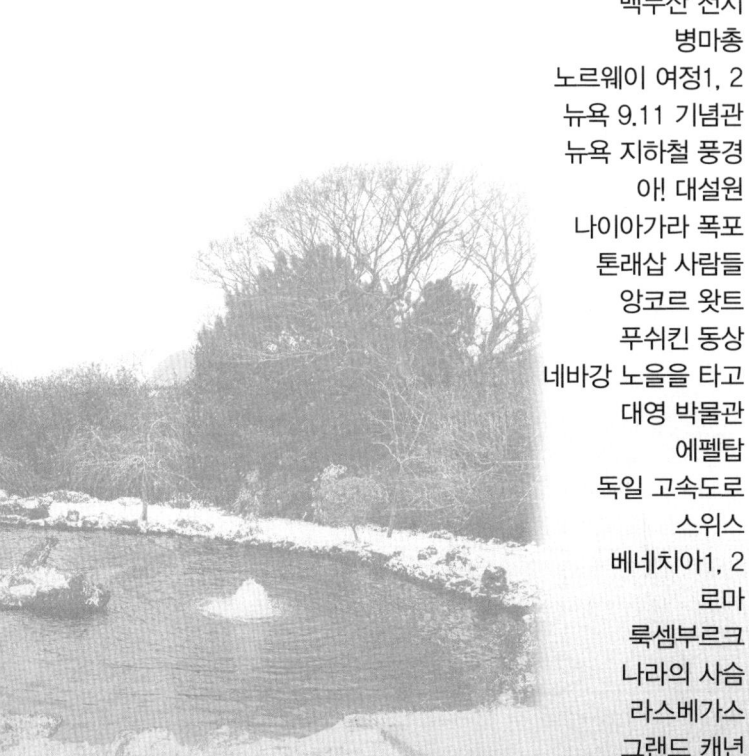

백두산 천지
병마총
노르웨이 여정1, 2
뉴욕 9.11 기념관
뉴욕 지하철 풍경
아! 대설원
나이아가라 폭포
톤래삽 사람들
앙코르 왓트
푸쉬킨 동상
네바강 노을을 타고
대영 박물관
에펠탑
독일 고속도로
스위스
베네치아1, 2
로마
룩셈부르크
나라의 사슴
라스베가스
그랜드 캐년

백두산 천지

딱 벌린 입안으로
천지(天池)가 들어온다

오천 년 겨레 역사
하나이게 이어보자

민족의 얼과 맥 이어
영원토록 기리자.

Baekdu-Mountain Sky Pond

The energy of the pond
rushes into my open mouth.

5,000 years of our history.
Let us continue as one

Connecting an vein of the nation
let's celebrate forever.

병마총

농부의 손에 의해
발견된 병마도용

역사적 무덤에서
진시황은 살아났고

황금알 역사 보물로
중국인은 살찐다.

Terracotta Warriors

Terracotta Warriors were
discovered by a farmer.

In the historical tomb,
Qin Shi Emperor survives.

The treasure of the golden egg
makes Chinese people fat.

노르웨이 여정1

만년설 폭포수에
어우러진 초원의 집

강물의 V자 계곡
빙하에 U자형은

음과 양 절경을 이룬
환상적인 피오르.

Norway Itinerary 1

Meadow house in harmony
with the ice cap waterfall.

V-shaped valley of the river
was U-shaped on the glacier.

It's superb view of yin and yang,
It is a fantastic fjord.

노르웨이 여정2

시침은 밤이지만
낮인 듯 훠~언하니

일몰의 시간 뒤에
일출을 보기 위해

희미한 백야의 밤을
보초 서듯 지켰다.

Norway Itinerary 2

The clock's hour hand points to the night.
But it's bright as if it's daytime.

After the time of sunset
to see a beautiful sunrise,

the time of the filmy white night,
I kept it like a sentry.

뉴욕 9.11 기념관

호수의 물결 따라
떠오르는 영상들이

새겨진 이름 위에
아련히 비춰오니

관광객 사이사이로
긴 사연을 전한다.

New York 9/11 Memorial

Along the waters of the lake
images that come to mind,

on the name of the deceased
the image is dimly displayed.

The Images among visitors
tell a long story to them.

뉴욕 지하철 풍경

오대양 육대주의
모든 종족 다 모였다

미소는 만국 언어
고운 마음 전해오고

오가는 눈빛만으로
지구촌은 하나다.

New York Subway Scene

The five oceans, six continents,
all the races gathered.

Smile is a Global language
each other send their kind heart.

With only the eyes that come and go
the global village is one.

아! 대설원
– 알프스 정상에서

한 마디 외침으로
넋을 잃고 바라본다.

햇살과 부딪히는
신비로운 선경(仙境)에서

산해봉 힘찬 기상이
온몸으로 스민다.

Ah! Great Snowfield
– At The Top of the Alps

Ah! with a single loud cry
I look at snowfield in awe.

In a mystical fairyland
colliding with sunlight,

the strong soul of the mountain peak
approaches all over body.

나이아가라 폭포

폭포가 포효하듯
굉음으로 소리친다

"가까이 오지말라
한 입으로 삼키리라"

시퍼런 서슬에 질려
물러서고 말았다.

Niagara Falls

Like a waterfall roaring
make an exclamation.

"Don't come approach to me
I will swallow you with one bite."

By that force approaching strongly
I eventually backed out.

톤래삽 사람들

아이들 놀이터는
넓디넓은 톤래삽* 호수

그곳이 생활 터전
그곳이 관광지네

문명의 이기 몰라도
자족하며 산다네

* 톤래삽 호수: 캄보디아에 있는 동양 최대의 호수로 수상 마을이 형성되어 있다.
It is the largest lake in the Orient in Cambodia and has a village floating on the water.

Tonlae Sap People

Tonlae Sap children's playground
is the vast Tonlae Sap* Lake

That place is the place of life,
that place is a tourist spot.

They don't know civilization,
but they live there happily.

앙코르 왓트*

인간의 우매함이
자신을 신격화해

불상한 백성들만
노역으로 숨졌으니…

돌덩이 하나하나에
원혼의 눈 박혔네.

---

* 앙코르 왓트: 수리아바르만 2세가 자신의 유해를 안치하고 상징적 종교로 비슈뉴 신과 자신을 영원히 동일시 할 수 있는 거대한 소우주의 건축물로 세운 것이다. 연인원 5만명으로 30년간 동원되었다.

Angkor Wat*

A human stupidity is
to make oneself a deify.

Only powerless people
died due to harder labor.

On each stone piled high toward the sky
is stuck the eyes of the ghoast .

* Angkor Wat : It was built as a gigantic microcosmic structure where King Suryavarman II enshrined his remains and could identify himself with Vishnu forever as a symbolic religion. It was mobilized for 30 years with fifthy thousand a year.

푸쉬킨 동상

손으로 턱을 괴고
무엇을 생각할까

싸늘한 일기탓에
콧물*이 흐르는 듯

저마다 기리는 시간
시심으로 채운다.

* 푸쉬킨 동상은 콧물이 흐른 흔적이 보인다.

Pushkin Statue

Rest your chin on your right hand
what do you think about.

because of the cold weather
As if runny nose* is flowing.

Everyone's feelings for Pushkin
are filled it with poetry's heart.

* The statue of Pushkin shows traces of runny nose.

네바강 노을을 타고

(우와~아 함성이 터졌다)

햇무리 수평선에
노을 되어 펼쳐지니

금실을 풀어논 듯
환상적인 물결 물결

네바강 노을을 타고
달려가는 시심(詩心)들.

Riding the Sunset on the Neva River

(Wow~ah, cheers broke out)

Sunbeam on the horizon
spreads out as the sunset.

As if the gold thread was released
fantastic water wave.

Hearts running riding the sunset
on the Neva River.

대영 박물관

세계의 옛 문화를
옮겨놓은 박물관은

제국의 옛 영화가
그대로 보이는 듯

승자의 만세 소리는
패자에겐 읍(泣)소리.

British Museum

The old cultures of the world were
moved to the British Museum.

The old glory of the empire
seems to be coming near .

The hurrah of the strong winner
was the cries of the losers.

에펠탑(la Tour Eiffel)

320m의 에펠탑은
철강구조 기념물로

불란스 혁명 100주년,
세계박람회를 위한 구조물,

찬란한 밤의 경치로
관광객을 부른다

* 에펠탑은 철강구조물로 3층까지 1652계단에
  2천5백개의 못이 박혀 무게가 1만톤이다

Eiffel Tower (La Tour Eiffel)

The 320m Eiffel Tower is
a steel structure monument.

It's a structure for the French
Revolution and the World's Fair.

The Tower attracts many tourists
with its glorious night views.

* The Eiffel Tower is a steel structure with 1652 steps to the third floor.
  It is studded with 2,500 nails and weighs 10,000 tons.

독일 고속도로

잘 닦인 고속도로
대통령을 감동시켜

두 김씨* 반대에도
일심으로 밀고 나가

이룩한 경부고속도로
경제 대국 초석 됐다.

* 경부고속도로 공사 당시 야당 지도자였던 김영삼 김대중이 극구 반대했다.
  사진을 보면 김대중은 공사장에 드러눕기도 했다.

German Highway

Germany's well-paved highways
impressed President Park Jeong-hui.

Even though the two Kims* opposed
single-mindedly pushed forward.

The highway of well-maintained kyeongbu
was the economic basis.

스위스

천혜의 자연경관
그림처럼 아름답다.

수돗물 바로 먹고
봄 여름 공존 터니

몽블랑 산꼭대기엔
진눈개비 날렸다.

Swiss

The natural scenery is
as beautiful as a painting.

I drink tap water right away
and there is no pollution.

A sleet fall on the top of Mont Blanc.
It's spring under the mountain

베네치아1

우리네 도시미화
새것으로 바꾸는데

물 위에 내려 앉은
낡은 집을 바라보며

연륜과 옛 모습대로
사랑함을 익힌다

Venice 1

Beautification of city,
we have changed it to new one

Looking at halfway of
an old house on the water,

looks the same as age and old things
I learn them to brag old things.

베네치아2

벽에는 낙서하나
지우지 아니하고

길가엔 쓰레기를
봉투채로 버려둔 채

그 자리, 있는 그대로
관광객을 맞는다.

Venice 2

On the old wall, graffiti are
there without erasing it.

There are many garbage bags
piled up on the roadside.

Waste is not cleaned up as it is,
Venice welcomes tourists proudly.

로마

'세계는 로마로부터'
옛 영광을 바라본다

수많은 문화유산
그대로 간직한 채

로마는 도시 전체가
그대로의 박물관.

Rome

'The world is from Rome' the word,
I look at the old glory.

Many cultural heritage,
they is keeping it as it is.

The city is the intact museum,
the whole city as it is.

룩셈부르크

'유럽의 골동품' 이라
절찬한 나폴레옹

작지만 알찬 나라
절벽 위의 천년 요새는

고성(古城)인 클레르보와
관광지의 중심지.

Luxembourg

"European Antiques"
Napoleon admired,

Small however rich country
the thousand-year fortress on Cliff,

The Clervaux is the old castle
which is center of tourism.

나라의 사슴

나라의 국립공원
사슴이 인사한다

과자를 던져주면
고맙다고 인사한다

어쩌면 사슴까지도
국민성을 닮은 듯.

Deer in Nara

In the Nara national park,
deers say hello to tourists.

If they throw the deer their cookies
The deer bows in gratitude.

Probably even the meek deers
It seem to resemble nation.

라스베가스

허허한 낮의 거리
사막 위 밤의 도시

땅거미 찾아들면
차(car) 물결, 사람 물결

화려한 라스베가스
밤의 거리 도박판.

Las Vegas

It is empty daytime street,
night city in the desert,

When the dusk comes on the street,
streets are car wave, people wave.

Las Vegas, the city in the desert is
gorgeous night street, gambling board.

그랜드 캐년

자연의 신비함에
마음까지 빨려들고

절묘한 그 전경에
창조주를 경외한다

조물주 모든 재주는
이 한 곳에 모인 듯

Grand Canyon

I was absorbed even my mind
in the mysteries of nature.

With that exquisite view,
I'm in awe of the Creator.

All talents of Creator God,
gathered in this one place.

제5부
일상의 소묘

초록이 비치네요
나비 정원
결국은
기분 따라
Beautiful Relaxing Music을 들으며
춤추는 능소화
신독(愼獨)
현대인의 나이
고향의 향
영상을 보며
Tim Janis의 영상 음악을 감상하며
공평한 기다림
카톡이 생명
시조의 세계화
송구영신
부활의 아침

초록이 비치네요.

저것 봐,
잔가지에 초록이 비치네요

사르르 올라오는
생명들의 연한 소리

자연의 귀한 작품이
태어나고 있어요. (2023.3.5.)

It's Green

Look at that,
the green reflects on the sprig of a willow.

I hear quietly the mellow
sound of life rising gently.

The precious work of the nature
is being born at this moment. (2023.3.5.)

나비 정원

드넓은 정원에는
꽃들이 만발하고

벌 나비 모여들어
잔치상을 올리네요

꽃 나라 나비 정원엔
행복 꽃도 피어요.

*우리 밭엔 제초제를 안 쓰기에 생물들의 천국이다.
* We do not use herbicides in our field, so it is a paradise for all things.

Butterfly Garden

Various flowers are in full bloom
in the extensive garden.

Bees and butterflies gather
to raise a opulent feast.

Happiness flowers also bloom
in our garden of flowers.

결국은

우리가 가꿔 가는
자연의 작품들은

행복을 키워내는
삶이 되는 길이기에

이 순간 기지개 켜는
새 생명을 보듬네.

In the End

These beautiful works of nature
that we cultivate well,

because it is our life and
duty that we protects the earth.

This moment, I embrace a new life
that is stretching here and there.

기분 따라

마음이 어두울 땐
해님이 불러주고

그 마음 밝아지면
바람이 불러 주어

하루해
밟고 지나간
추억들이 새롭다.

Follow the Mood

When my heart is dark for nothing
the bright sun is calling me.

When that heart brightens by smile
The wind calls that mind again.

Stepping on a daily routine
and I miss the memories.

Beautiful Relaxing Music을 들으며
− 영상 음악에 들다

경치가 아름답다
음악이 아름답다

마음이 평안하다
꽃들이 인사한다

보던 책
한끝 접고서
영상 속에 빠진다.

Listening to Beautiful Relaxing Music
− Listen to Video Music

The scenery is beautiful
the music is soft and sweet.

I have a peaceful mind
flowers beckon forward to me.

Reading book
with one end folded
I fall into the video.

춤추는 능소화

사모의 정이 넘쳐
불타는 송이송이

빗줄기 내리쳐도
꺼질 줄 모르더니

무위의
손을 잡고서
춤을 추는 능소화

Dancing Trumpet Creeper

Overflowing with loving heart
burning trumpet creeper flowers,

Even if it rains down on it,
burning flowers don't turn off.

Oh! holding its hands of inaction
trumpet creeper is dancing.

신독(愼獨)

습관은 제2천성
지나쳐 듣지 마라

무심히 한 언행은
습관에서 오게 되니

예사람
신독(愼獨)의 자세
새겨 봄도 좋을 듯.

Be Careful When Alone

Habit is second nature
do not overhear lightly.

Words and actions done carelessly,
It comes from normal habits

The old man,
attitude of alone(愼獨),
It would be nice to engrave it.

현대인의 나이

아무리 숫자 세며
나이를 밝혀봐도

숫자는 숫자일 뿐
모습 따라 건강 따라

나이는
벼이삭처럼
익어가는 중이다.

Modern Age

No matter how many numbers
Even if you reveal your age

Numbers are just numbers
according to appearance, health

Ages is
like rice ears in the rice field
and ripening naturally.

고향의 향

꽃처럼 아름다운
빨갛게 익은 감과

돌담을 돌아들면
구수한 숭늉 냄새

아련한
고향의 향이
가을볕에 따습다.

Scent of Home

It is the red ripe persimmon
beautiful as a flower.

If you go around the stone wall
savory '*sung-nyung' flavor.

Indistinct
the fragrance of home
is warm in the autumn sun.

* 'sung-nyuo' *:water boiled with burned rice

영상을 보며

우주의 삼라만상
영상 속에 다 있는데

무엇이 또 있을까
반짝이는 별 너머엔

아마도
하늘나라가
그 너머엔 있겠지.

Watching the Video

All creation of universe,
they are in the video

I wonder what else is there,
beyond the twinkling stars.

Well may be,
Elysium I miss
will be beyond the other side.

Tim Janis의 영상 음악을 감상하며

음악과 어울리는
자연이 아름답다

새들은 새들끼리
꽃들은 꽃들끼리

어울려
함께 펼치는
영상 속의 별(別)세계

Listening to the Video Music of Tim Janis

Nature getting along with
the music is beautiful.

Birds get along each other,
flowers match each other.

 A well mached
spreading together
It's another world in video. (2022.12.4.)

공평한 기다림

어릴 땐 아이들이
엄마를 기다린다

그 아이 어른 되어
엄마 아빠 된 후에는

그 엄만
할머니 되어
아이들을 기다린다. (2022.12.23.)

The Fair Wait

When children are juvenile,
they are waiting for mother.

Those children become adults,
After becoming a mom and father,

the mother
become grandmother,
she is waiting for children.

카톡이 생명

날마다 카톡 검토
여기저기 빨간 숫자

코로나 팬데믹에
마음만은 가까운 듯

그 옛날
시대였다면
어떻게들 견딜까?

Kakao Talk is Life

I check my Kakao Talk,
there are red numbers everywhere.

In the Covid-19 pandemic
It seems that only heart is close.

The old days,
If it was the era,
how can we stand Covid-19?

시조의 세계화

풍성한 시조 꽃이
홀씨로 승화하여

훠-얼 훠-얼 날아가서
자유를 만끽하며

단숨에
태평양 건너
시조 밭을 일구렴.

Globalization of Sijo

Everyone's sijo flower
sublimates into a spore,

huh-uh-uh-uh fly away
enjoying the freedom,

at a whack,
across the pacific,
please cultivate the Sijo field.

송구영신

지나간 3년여가 30년을 기다린 듯
저마다 셀폰 들고 제야의 종 기다리니
정녕코 하무뭇하다 추억 또한 그립네

그 해(年)가 그해지만 새해라 일컫듯이
그 해(陽)가 그 해인데 해돋이 소원비네
저마다 새해 소망을 해님에게 아뢰네.

날마다 쏘아대는 김정은의 헛발질에
휴전선 허리부터 철조망 지뢰까지
새해엔 말끔히 씻겨 평화공원 되소서.

(2022.12.31.)

Welcome the New Year

The past three years seem to have
waited for thirty years,
Each one waits for the bell of
the New Year's Eve holding a phone,
Certainly, It is really glad,
I also miss the memories.

The year is the year, but
as it is called the New Year,
The sun is the sun, however,
people make their wishes to sun.
Everyone tells the sun their wishes
for the new year of the hope.

At the miss step of Kim Jong-un
shooting almost every day,
from the armistice line
to the barbed wire and mine,
the New Year, those are washed clean;
let it be the peaceful park.

부활의 아침
  – 부활절을 맞아

부활절 신새벽에 새 생명 태어나요
새순이 파릇파릇 힘차게 돋아나고
성도의 기도 소리가 하늘 문에 닿네요.

파릇한 새순들이 힘차게 두 손 뻗고
간절한 기도 소리 하늘 문이 열리네요
정의와 사랑의 기도 주님 전에 닿아요.

부활의 기적 앞에 성도는 두 손 모아
기도와 찬송으로 주님을 맞이하니
그윽한 믿음의 향기 온 세상에 가득해요.

나 또한 주님 말씀 심중에 새기면서
어린이 마음으로 두 손 모아 기도하며
천국 문 바라보면서 부활절을 맞아요.

생명이 태어났던 부활절 이 아침에
주님이 승리했던 부활의 깃발 들고
성도들 찬송 소리에 부활의 꽃 피워요.

(2023.3.29. 복음신문 게재)

Resurrection Morning
― Easter Day

At the new dawn of Easter,
the life is born by relife
New shoot sprout vigorously
freshly green here and there
The prayers of the saints reach to
the gates of heaven garden.

Green shoots vigorously
stretch out their hands powerfully.
The sound of earnest prayer,
 like the opening of the door,
Saints prayers of justice and love
reach before the Lord the God.

In front of the miracle of resurrection,
saints put their hands together
We greet the Lord the God
with prayer and praise of believers
The deep scents of faith of the saints
fill all over the world.

Engraving the words of the Lord
within myself deep heart,
Put my hands together and
pray with the heart of a child
By drawing the image of the Lord
celebrate Easter today.

On this Easter morning
when a new life was born,
raising the banner of
resurrection that the Lord won,
the flower of resurrection blooms
the sound of the angel's trumpet.

(2023.3.29.)

〈부록〉　　　　저자 이정자의 이력

1. 문단활동
1990년 문학과 의식 신인상 수상(평론 부문)
1990년 시조문학 제1회 추천
1991년 시조문학 제2회 추천
1992년 봄호(계간70호)시조문학 천료
2006년 제6회 올해의 시조문학작품상 수상
2008년 (사)한국시조문학진흥회 주최 동양대학교 시조문학 특강
2008년 10월 18일 한국서학회 주최 예술의 전당에서 학술세미나
　　　"시조의 이해" 강연
2009년 (사)한국서학회 주최 시조로 꾸미는 아름다운 한글서예전에서 시조
　　　100편을 선정하다.(예술의전당 내 서울서예박물관에서 2009년 9
　　　월 8일 – 9월 13일)
2009년6월13일 단양군 역동 우탁 기념사업회 주관 학술발표(우탁의 생애와 학문)
2012년 고산시조문학상 대상 수상
2013년 하운문학상 수상(평론)
2013년 10월 12일 한국시조문학진흥회 주관 학술 세미나 발표(교통대 중
　　　앙도서관. 주제 : 이태극론, 「월하의 사랑과 이별 그리고 회한」)
2011.12.21. 『한국시조문학』 창간
2011년–2013년 : 한국시조문학 발행인 및 편집인
　　　(사)국제펜 한국본부 이사 및 번역위원 (사)한국시조시인협회 자문위
　　　원, (사)한국시조협회 자문위원, 한국문인협회회원, 시조문학 운영위
　　　원, 시조문학 집필전문위원(역임), 시조문학 편집위원, 풀꽃동인 고문.

　　　　사단법인 한국시조문학진흥회 이사장 (2011-2013)
　　　　이대동창문인회 회장(2018-2020.5) (현) 고문
　　　　시조문학 제3대 발행 및 편집인(2022 여름호 -)
　　　　(사)한국시조문학협회 이사장(2023-)
* 문학상
　　　　평론신인상(문학과 의식사 1990)
　　　　시조문학작품상(2006), 고산윤선도문학상(2012)
　　　　역동문학상(2015), 이화문학상(2017), 한하운문학평론상(2012)
　　　* UPLI(세계계관시인협회)KC(한국위원회)번역상(2017,국제화에 앞서가는 시인), 제1회 일두시조문학상(2020), 한국시조문학백년상(2022).

2. 저서
1) 학술서적
　(1) 한국 시가의 아니마 연구 (백문사, 1996)
　(2) 시조문학연구론 (국학자료원, 2003)
　(3) 글쓰기의 이론과 실제 (한올출판사, 2003)
　(4) 대화와 화술(국학자료원, 2003)
　(5) 논술문과 논문 작성법(새미, 2004)
　(6) 시와 시조 창작론 (국학자료원, 2004)
　(7) 글쓰기의 길잡이(국학자료원, 2005)
　(8) 말과 글(한올출판사, 2006)
　(9) 제정공 이달충 문학(국학자료원, 2006)
　(10) 명심보감 편저(한올출판사, 2008)
　(11) 고전의 샘에 마음을 적시다(국학자료원, 2009)
　(12) 시조 한 수에 역사가 숨쉰다(한국학술정보(주), 2009)

(13) 현대시조, 정격으로의 길(국학자료원, 2009)

(14) 사고와 표현(한올출판사, 2011)

(15) 한 수의 시조에 역사가 살아있다(국학자료원, 2011)

(16) 문학의 이해(한올출판사, 2012년문광부 우수학술도서선정)

(17) 글쓰기와 프레젠테이션(한올출판사, 2014)

(18) 현대시조문학사(국학자료원, 2014)

2) 자유시집

(1) 하늘의 이슬로 된 진주이고자(백문사, 1996)

(2) 영의 눈이 뜨일 때 (한결, 2001)

(3) 마음의 풍경(새미, 2008)

3) 시조집

제1시조집, 가을 꽃 여울 타고 (토방, 1996)

제2시조집, 마음의 창을 열면(한결, 2000)

제3·4시조집, 기차여행 – 사계의 노래(새미, 2005)

제5시조집, 시조의 향기(새미, 2007)

제6·7시조집, 자연의 곳집을 열고 – 부엉이 바위(새미, 2009)

제8시조집, 내 안의 섬 (새미, 2014)

제9·10시조집, 아버지의 산 – 전원일기(국학자료원 2017)

제11·12시조집, 눈을 들어 산을 보라 – 문득 바라본 창밖 그림(2022.넥센)

제13시조집, 뿌리를 찾아서(도서출판 조은 2023)

4) 번역시조집

* 한영시조 『빗방울 A Raindrop』(국학자료원 (2015. 9)

* 이정자의 단시조 선1 『내 안의 섬 An Island in My Mind』(2014. 새미)

* 이정자의 단시조 선2 『아버지의 산 Father's Mountain』(2017.국학자료원)

* 이정자의 한영 단시조 선집 『민들레 Dandelion』(2021.넥센)

* 이정자의 5개국어 단시조선집 『민들레 Dandelion』 (2022, 한국문학신문)
* 이정자의 한영시조집 『뿌리를 찾아서 Looking for My Roots』

5) 에세이집:
   (1) 풀은 마르고 꽃은 시드나 (한결, 2001)
   (2) 당신의 인생도 업그레이드 해보라(국학자료원, 2006)

3. 논문

1) 고산시가의 미학적 연구, 석사논문 (이화여대, 교육대학원, 1975)
2) 이달충 문학연구 – 한시를 중심으로 – 석사논문(건국대 대학원, 1992)
3) 고시가의 아니마 연구 박사논문(건국대 대학원, 1995)
4) 구지가의 공간적 연구(건대 대학원 논문집, 1994)
5) 한용운과 타고르의 영향관계–님의 침묵과 기탄잘리 원정 등–(대학원 논문집, 1994)
6) 문정공 이달충 문학연구(대학원논문집, 1991)
7) 밝혀진 조운의 면모와 그의 작품 연구(시조문학, 1991)
8) 조남령 연구(시조문학, 1991)
9) 추사 김정희의 언간에 나타난 찬도 생활 면모(흐름동인 제1집. 1991)
10) 김현승과 R.M.Rilke와의 영향관계(흐름동인 제2집 1992)
11) 김기림과 T.S Eliot의 영향관계(흐름동인 제4집 1995)
12) 이문열과 헤르만 헷세의 영향관계 (흐름동인제5집1996)
    – 그해 겨울과 크눌프, 우리들의 일그러진 영웅과 데미안 등 –
13) 동인시화에 나타난 서거정의 시론(중원논문집, 1998)
14) 예덕 선생전 연구(대학원 발표 논문)
15) 춘일 소양강행 차운시 연구 (중원 문학, 2002)
16) 고전시가에 나타난 동화적 요소(동화와 번역, 2004)
17) 향가에 나타난 동화적 요소(동화와 번역, 2005)

18) 역동 우탁 연구(우탁학술제 발표, 2009. 6. 13)
19) 한하운 시에 나타난 시조 율격론(한국문단, 2012)
20) 이태극론, 월하의 사랑과 이별 그리고 회한 (2013, 한국시조문학 5호)
21) 역동 우탁의 시대정신과 시조의 방향성(2018. 한국시조문학 14호)
21) 신사임당과 육영수 여사 비교 고찰(2020. 한국시조문학 봄호)
22) 일두 정여창의 문학 고찰(2021. 한국시조문학 봄호)
23) 역동 선생과 선비정신에 대한 고찰(2021 .한국시조문학 여름호)
24) 기타

4. 평론 · 비평

1) 고산시가 미학론 (계간)문학과 의식 (1990. 여름호)
2) 기청의 연첩시조에 대한 반론 (자유문학 2006. 여름호)
3) 시조의 형식 파괴가 발전일까(시조문학 2006. 가을호)
4) 조세용 시집 [사향(思鄕)]발문에 부쳐(해동문학, 2007. 가을호)
5) 현대시조의 당면과제에 대한 제언(시조문학 2008. 여름호)
6) 시조의 세계화를 꿈꾼다(조선일보 2008. 9. 9)
7) 한글학회100주년에 시조를...(해동문학 2008. 겨울호)
8) 현대시조의 변격과 파격(시조문학, 2009. 가을호)
9) 송귀영 시조에 나타난 작가의식(시조문학, 2012. 여름호)
10) 원용우 시조에 나타난 작가의식(팔순 기념 문집)
11) 신웅순 시조에 나타난 작가의식 (정년 퇴임 문집)
12) 임병웅 시조 평설 : 시조집 『산마루에 올라』 (2021. 한국시조문학, 봄호)
13) 김신아 시조 평설 : 시조집 『산수유 마을』 (2021. 한국시조문학가을호)
14) 김인자 시조 평설 : 시조집 『삶,꽃으로 피다』 (2021. 한국시조문학겨울호)♣
15) 고순옥의 시조 평설 : 시조집 『달빛 요정』 (2023.)

Lee Jeongja's 13th Sijo Collection (2023)

In Search of The Root

Written by Jeongja Lee

Jo-Eun Publishing House